HORSE BREEDS

AMERICAN MINIATURE HORSE

BY LIBBY WILSON

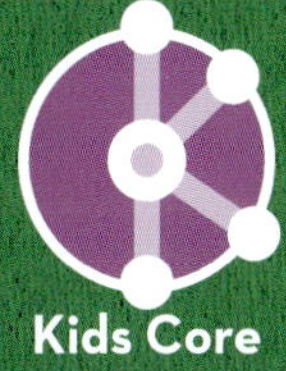

Kids Core

An Imprint of Abdo Publishing
abdobooks.com

abdobooks.com

Published by Abdo Publishing, a division of ABDO, PO Box 398166, Minneapolis, Minnesota 55439.

Printed in the United States of America, North Mankato, Minnesota.
052025
092025

Cover Photo: Shutterstock Images
Interior Photos: Dan Henry/Chattanooga Times Free Press/AP Images, 4–5; Gentle Carousel Miniature Therapy Horses, 6; Ann E. Parry/Alamy, 8; Vera Zinkova/Shutterstock Images, 10–11, 14; Charles Hewitt/Picture Post/Hulton Archive/Getty Images, 13; Tom Nebbia/The Image Bank Unreleased/Getty Images, 16; Abramova Kseniya/Shutterstock Images, 18–19, 20, 28–29; Studio Ayutaka/Shutterstock Images, 21; Shutterstock Images, 22, 23; Mira Oberman/AFP/Getty Images, 25; Slawik, C./juniors@wildlife/Juniors Bildarchiv GmbH/Alamy, 26

Editor: Marie Pearson
Series Designer: Ryan Gale

Library of Congress Control Number: 2024948983

Publisher's Cataloging-in-Publication Data

Names: Wilson, Libby, author.
Title: American miniature horse / by Libby Wilson
Description: Minneapolis, Minnesota: Abdo Publishing, 2026 | Series: Horse breeds | Includes online resources and index.
Identifiers: ISBN 9781098297459 (lib. bdg.) | ISBN 9798384919971 (ebook)
Subjects: LCSH: Miniature horses--Juvenile literature. | Horses--Juvenile literature. | Horse breeds--Juvenile literature. | Zoology--Juvenile literature.
Classification: DDC 636.109--dc23

CONTENTS

Magic has brought joy to many people.

SHE'S MAGIC

Magic is a black American miniature horse with bright blue eyes. She is visiting a woman at a home for elderly people. The woman has lived there for three years, but she has not spoken since she moved in.

Magic works with the Ocala Police Department during reading programs at schools.

The woman pets Magic. She says, "Isn't she beautiful?"

A staff member tears up. She never expected to hear her patient speak. "I love you," the staff member tells the woman.

The woman replies, "I love you too."

Magic has worked a miracle for the resident. The woman continues to talk after Magic's visit. Magic is a therapy horse. She visits cancer patients and sick children. She brings comfort to survivors of hurricanes and fires. Some people find comfort in hugging her. Magic has received dozens of awards for the good she does for people.

Therapy Horse Training

Miniature horses used for therapy train for two years before making visits. They practice going up and down stairs and riding in elevators. They learn to calmly handle unexpected sounds such as shouts, alarms, and sirens. And they learn to use the bathroom only outside.

American miniature horses can make good children's horses.

A Miniature Breed

The American miniature horse is a light horse breed. Light horses are those bred for riding, such as Arabians and Thoroughbreds. They are slim, athletic, and elegant. American miniature horses are bred to look like tiny riding horses. Minis, however, should be ridden only by people under 70 pounds (32 kg). Like dogs and cats, they are considered companion animals.

The American miniature horse is quickly gaining popularity. There are more than 240,000 American miniature horses worldwide. There's lots to love about this little breed!

Explore Online

Visit the website below. Does it give any new information about Magic that wasn't in Chapter One?

Magic

abdocorelibrary.com/american-miniature-horse

People teach their miniature horses tricks for shows or fun.

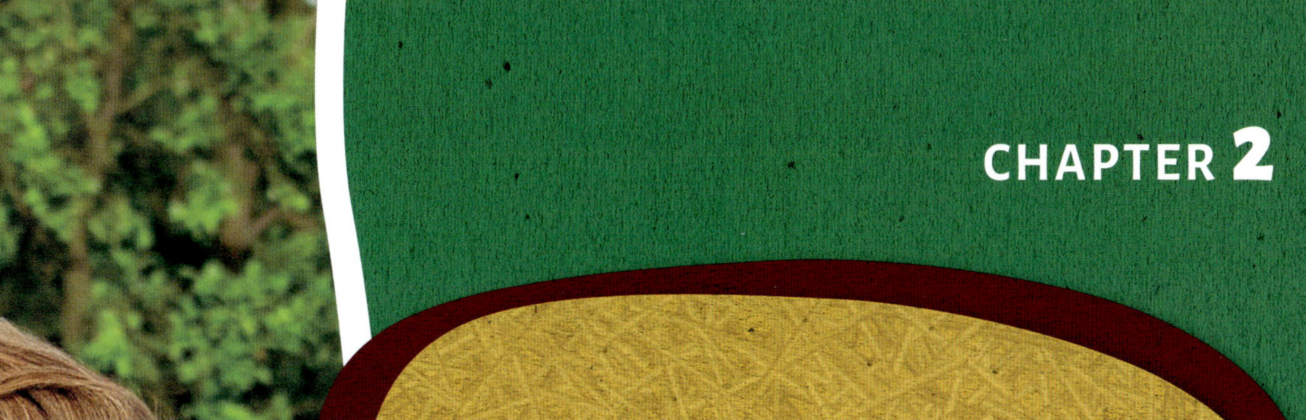

CHAPTER 2

MINIATURE HORSE HISTORY

The first record of a miniature horse was in 1650 CE. France's King Louis XIV kept them in his zoo of unusual animals. Other European royals kept them as pets. Minis also performed in traveling circuses.

Later, Europeans put minis to work in coal mines. In the early 1800s, children worked long hours in underground mines. They pushed tubs of coal through narrow shafts. It was hard, dangerous work. In 1842, the United Kingdom passed a child labor law. Children were no longer allowed to work in the pit mines. Miniature horses were among the horses that replaced them. They lived underground, spending their lives in darkness.

Coming to America

The first miniature horse came to the United States in about 1888. Many others followed. They worked in Appalachian coal mines until the 1950s. Then mines began to replace ponies

The small horses that were used in coal mines were called pit ponies.

with machines. Horse farmers began to breed their smallest horses to sell as pets. This started the breeding program of today's American miniature horse.

Breeders used different types of horses to develop the features they wanted minis to have.

Breeders mixed in many types of horses. The Shetland pony is one of the American miniature horse's **foundation** breeds. Thoroughbreds and high-stepping hackney ponies brought athletic movement and a fine build. Pintos and Appaloosas added colorful patterns. Tiny Falabellas gave the horse its small size.

Falabellas

American miniature horse breeders use the world's tiniest horse breed to reduce the size of their minis. Falabellas average 32 inches (81 cm) tall at the shoulder. The breed came from Argentina. They are known for their flashy coats and graceful movements. They often live 40 to 45 years.

In the late 1900s, people started showing their miniature horses for prizes such as trophies and ribbons.

Breed **registries** were organized in the 1970s. The American Shetland Pony Club started the American Miniature Horse Registry (AMHR). A registry called the American Miniature Horse Association (AMHA) also formed. It published a breed standard for the American miniature horse. A breed standard describes the ideal appearance and personality of a breed. The AMHA's goal is to create the smallest possible horse with the ideal proportions of full-sized light horse breeds.

Further Evidence

Look at the website below. Does it give any new evidence to support Chapter Two?

Horse Breeds

abdocorelibrary.com/american-miniature-horse

A miniature horse is about the same weight as a mastiff.

CHAPTER 3

LIVING WITH A MINI

American miniature horses are the size of large dogs. The AMHA registers minis up to 34 inches (86 cm) tall. The AMHR registers minis up to 38 inches (97 cm). Adult minis average 150 to 250 pounds (68–113 kg). They come in all colors and patterns.

A newborn miniature horse foal weighs about 20 pounds (9 kg). It is 16 to 21 inches (41–53 cm) tall.

The difference between horses, ponies, and miniature horses is mostly size. But ponies have shorter legs, wider necks, and stockier bodies than miniature and light horses. Ponies also have thicker coats, tails, and manes.

Health

Miniature horses require much of the same care as other horses. But minis do have some special needs. **Obesity** is a common problem for minis.

American Miniature Horse Height

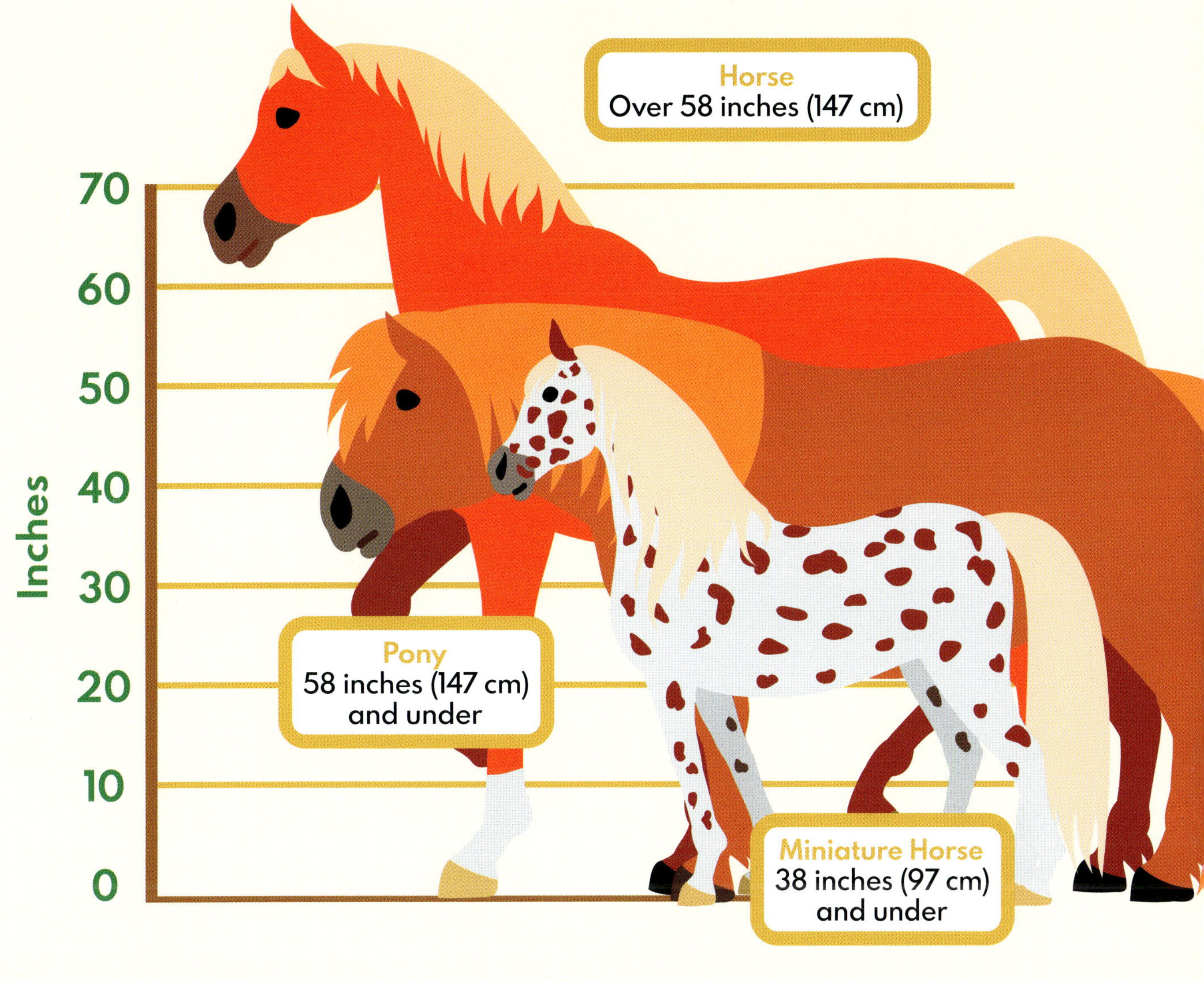

Minis are measured from the ground to the point on their back where the mane stops growing. Ponies and horses are measured from the ground to the top of their withers. Withers is the name of the bony ridge over the shoulders that marks the tallest point of the back.

Minis can get exercise playing with other minis in a field.

They love to eat! Because they are so small, they don't need much food per day. A lot of health problems can be avoided by keeping minis at an ideal weight.

Daily exercise is necessary. A **pasture** is needed for **grazing** and running. Minis are healthiest if they get to run outside every day.

For their safety, miniature horses are sometimes kept in separate herds from large horses.

One acre (0.4 ha) is plenty of room for several minis. Some experts say minis should be kept separate from large horses. A big horse could hurt a mini if they start playing and kicking.

Teeth

Dental problems are more common for minis than larger horses. The same size and number of teeth grow in a smaller mouth. Dental problems can lead to poor chewing. This may cause a stomach issue called colic.

Minis are at risk of dwarfism. This condition passes from parents to offspring. It causes unusually small size and **deformities**. Dwarfism is less common now than before. But matings between minis should be done by people who know how to avoid it.

Miniature Fun

Miniature horses are active companions. They pull carts and run obstacle courses. Minis compete in driving and jumping events. They play with fitness balls, walk in parades, and learn tricks such as bowing. Minis have even learned to paint and lead fitness classes.

Minis are good for therapy work. Many form bonds with the people they visit. Minis can see

Minis can work for many more years than guide dogs because they live much longer.

people who are allergic to dogs. They are small enough to be transported in cars. Some minis work as service animals. They are trained to help people with disabilities. For example, some are used as guide animals for the blind.

Minis can make loving companions for children and adults.

American miniature horses are bred to be smart, curious, and gentle. Most are happiest just being with their owner. They want to be part of whatever the owner is doing. They are cooperative and easy to train. Owners love their miniature horses!

Karen Rudolph breeds world champion American miniature horses. She says:

> I am drawn to their huge personalities. I enjoy the grooming and the prep time involved with showing them. . . . I also love to share my little horses with others.

Source: "Small but Mighty: Discover the World of the Miniature Horse." *Cheshire Horse*, 19 Mar. 2020, blog.cheshirehorse.com. Accessed 6 Nov. 2024.

What's the Big Idea?

Read this quote carefully. What is its main idea? Explain how the main idea is supported by details.

BREED TRAITS

Coat with any colors or patterns

Fine mane and tail

Long, slender neck
Slim, muscular body
Straight, athletic legs

Glossary

deformities
body parts that have grown in ways that can cause challenges

foundation
something used at the beginning as a building block

grazing
feeding on land with grass or crops

obesity
a disease that comes from having too much body fat

pasture
an area of land with grass or crops where animals can feed

registry
an official list or record of individuals who belong to a breed

Online Resources

To learn more about American miniature horses and other horses, visit our free resource websites below.

Visit **abdocorelibrary.com** or scan this QR code for free Common Core resources for teachers and students, including vetted activities, multimedia, and booklinks, for deeper subject comprehension.

Visit **abdobooklinks.com** or scan this QR code for free additional online weblinks for further learning. These links are routinely monitored and updated to provide the most current information available.

Learn More

My Book of Horses and Ponies. DK, 2024.

Pearson, Marie. *Horse Behavior.* Abdo, 2024.

Ventura, Marne. *Horses.* Abdo, 2023.

Index

About the Author

Libby Wilson has loved books and reading her entire life. She enjoys researching and finding interesting facts to share with readers. Her favorite topics are nature, history, and inspirational people. She lives in Pennsylvania and North Carolina with her husband and golden retriever.